# The Shattered Mirror

by

## M. C. Rush

# Acknowledgments

I would like to thank the editors of the following journals and websites for first publishing some of the poems collected here.

*300 Days of Sun*: "The Spellcasters," "Global Warming"

*Better: Culture & Lit*: "Dissensus"

*Breakwater Review*: "Sex"

*Picayune Literary Magazine*: "Universal Translator"

*Shadowtrain*: "The Flaw"

*The Bicycle Review*: "Critic," "Critic 2"

*The Chaffey Review*: "Lusus Indorum"

*The Fieldstone Review*: "Elegy for Edges"

*The Tulane Review*: "The Wisdom of the Crowd"

*Word Riot*: "Amends"

All Faith is false, all Faith is true:
    Truth is the shattered mirror strown
In myriad bits; while each believes his
    little bit the whole to own.

Richard Francis Burton,
*The Kasidah of Haji Abdu El-Yezdi*

# Contents

# We Begin

We begin to be,
we change,
we end.

We begin
to be change,
we end.

We begin,
to be, we change,
we end.

We begin
to be, we change
to end.

# Amends

There can be no restitution
without an initial theft, so steal
outrageous takings:  air, sunlight,
more stars than you can count,
the eye of a smiling woman.
Then return everything,
barely tasted, merely tried,
set it all aside and run unburdened
to the next temptation waiting
to be named, waiting to be claimed.

# A poem's

an eddy of love in
a cracked cauldron of indifference,
indistinct toxic ink, precipitated spice

things get darker the longer the sun shines
but still – the light the bright the warm!

one blind blue eye in the old white beard of sky

get the wordparrots out of your mouth,
the thoughtmyna out of your mind

— to cage a songbird with its song
is wrong, is wrong —

red ant, black ant, beggar ant, grief's
drip-drying eyes, eager to owl

take a little from *everybody*!

vigilante vigils and excuses profuse, the oldspapers,
inaugural love, wars of spoil, and the monster's monster

neither yes nor no
and yes and no

give it all back to the world
and let the world choose
what to use, what to lose

# Perpetual

practicing wishcraft
in spaces uncontrolled, uncurated

refusing to be surprised
by familiar oddities

an adjustment of constraints,
a rearrangement of coercions

accumulating grievances,
dissipating attunement

to know what others are afraid to know
and then to say it

closed can't learn,
open leaks identity

everything may be denied
but the perception of illusion

# Hang On

The purpose of artifice is not to shame nature,
but to enhance her.  Your focus and your attunement.
Don't settle for interesting where true is available.
So much effort spent expressing the false.
So many suspicious of the nutritious.
What limits, Proteus? What do we want
but to rise above sameness while evading blame?
Too many people position themselves
to be hurt by people who are right.
You must let someone break
something before they'll understand
breakage.  It's hard.  And you
must let them choose
what to break.  So hard.

# Spring-Heeled Drone

You invite me to join the discretion,
to try to unnotice it.
Looking with eyes of no shadow,
no light, you ask me to love
the unutterable, the ostent
decreased, deceased, inauspicious
ambiguities, glimpses of distortion
soaking up the tropes, wrecked
dodecahedrons, barcode barricades,
the postprandial predilections
of cosmopolitan recidivists, idolaters
of union, memories of memories, the better
parrots, deformed by denial, proximity
to models, the tyranny of precision,
meticulous maliciousness, an itch to glitch,
ubiquitous fomites, spring-heeled drones,
the rapture of rupture, unless,
I guess, penultimatum, plurivalent,
the ever-emptier sea.
The unexpected is unfair;
the predictable, unbearable.

# The Tautology

I think, therefore I am.

Except that I don't—
I occur when thoughts are produced
by cause-and-effect processes
in a physical substrate.

When thoughts don't occur, I am not
(though the substrate may, for a while,
continue and renew).

"I think" presumes "I am"
or, reduced for simplicity, "I."

I am what observes thinking
and remembers some of it
(but memory, too, is just thought).

And since observation is thought,
it's just thinking about thinking,
or, thinking.

So who am I?  And am I?

# Wish

I wish I were a feral child
seven feet tall
and hidden in hair and dirt.

I'd live among stones above forest
and sing with the deep water
of the movements of silvery fish

and the moon, and wish
to soon find others, like me,
hairy, dirty, and wild.

# Available

I have made myself available
[for adventure]
[for special assignment]
[to be called upon to help someone in need]
[to do something meaningful].

I am not encumbered as others are,
am free in a way they can't match.
(They may have ways of their own.)

*This wasn't easy, dammit!*
Don't think it was.

I have made myself an outcast,
exiled from everyone,
and I can live with that, I guess.
It was a good idea at the time.
(There may have been better ones.)

I have made myself.
But if I am going to be called upon,
it had better be soon:
it's afternoon.

# Demon Is Human Drained of Love

Every generation
discovers its perfidy

and thinks
to have invented evil

in the tyranny
of custom and culture,

narrative necessities
subject to connotative rot,

an amalgam of atrocity
both static and erratic.

The temptation is to mythologize the mundane
to spin meaning from pain.

Is madness deviation from the norm
or deviation from reality?

Pressure issuing
from a fissure of frustration?

People would rather be lied to than ignored,
be ridiculed than unremarked.

Someone who goes too long unheard or unheeded
is at risk of impersonating the impersonal,

of settling for silence.
Not all can perform in solitary harmony.

We make noise to be noticed.
We long to be revered or reviled.

# Erotic Amalgam

Falling in love is autoerotic.
To inhibit or inhabit.

Put all the woe in the salt,
see all the joy in the surge.

The sea is the same.
Lurid, lucid.

What is hope but desire,
its fire diminished?

We are the snaste,
not the flame.

# Reciprocity

as futile
as seagulls
in parking lots

lyrical reciprocity
in hot pursuit
of mirages
of cool serenity

precious false promises
that shrivel
under one fire eye
one icy one

even language
the best friend
false friend
leaves one behind
leaves one

obligates
through obfuscation

an inheritance of instance
squandered to irrelevance

# Saving the World

Go out,
live,
add your tale to the library of the illiterates.

Hero lite,
standing up for those who won't stand up for themselves
rather than those who can't.

The credible threats of the craven
hedging the bets of compassion
with a lascivious civility, with elicited criticism.

Under the rosy moon of dawn
disarm some bombs,
militants, mutants,

media-steeped mania-junkies,
*coup-contrecoup*
along the thin line

that marks the massive chasm
between.

At what level do we not perform?
We're marauders tamed to consumers.

Even simple things are extravagant.
Items of comparable quality may not be equivalent.

The unique is glorious but, ultimately, insignificant.
Only the reproducible can really matter.

Which currency buys happiness?
Chance, justice, or unhappiness?

# Impasse

Look too closely at words
and all you will see are shadows.
Look too closely at anything
and all you will see are shadows.

When I see a good thing, I want it.
But is it good that I should have it?
When I see a bad thing, I avoid it.
But in so doing, do I feed it?

I don't want to get what I deserve,
I deserve to get what I want.
So I do want to get what I deserve,
I guess.  And to deserve what I want.

The music I never heard,
the food I never tasted,
the people I never met,
everything I missed.

Don't just tell me what you think I need to know—
tell me everything.
Don't just give me what you think I need—
give me everything.

Look too closely at shadows
and you won't see anything.

# Contrapasso

there are no things but in ideas

unconscious deities
proposing purpose

the shine of the shrine
recognition and reward

all in all, all out of all
the obsession with pattern

excess reduced to essence
condition and duration

I never said
I never would

my friends are all oxymorons,
outliers

focus is precious

# All I Want

I want what I have
and I want what I don't have.

I want what I will have
and I want what I won't have.

Let me have it,
what I want,
when I want it.

That's all I want.

# The Persistence of Fiction

It is easier to open to the entire natural world
than to the society of a single person.

How often, it seems, I am estrangered
by those near me.

Those who perform love as satire.

How flexible our design,
that we can care or not care,
aid or not aid,
do or refrain from doing!

Should the body pity or envy the mind
that it is never naked?

Without intent, there are no mistakes.

The best wine is just polluted water.

The metaphorical is always preferable
to the metaphysical.

What happens,
our reaction to what happens,
our relation to what happens,
our stories about what happens.

The bravura of text
unscrupulously
textured into scripture.

Exploiting locally nonrandom phenomena
in a random environment.

How do you respond to the 20th Century
during which it was settled
that everything should die?

# Diversions

Someone says "Look."
Someone says "Listen."

Directing your attention
differently.

Look, you know it's not the same.
Listen, I'm not going to say it again.

Useless ritual
whose point's to soothe.

There's something wrong with you
if you find lies easier to believe than the truth.

We all like them better, sometimes,
but you can't just believe what you like.

Words worried into wards
against *l'appel du vide*.

I meet so few people,
and all of them the wrong ones.

Content to adorn their silence
with raucous baubles.

Consciousness derives poetry.
But consciousness *is* a poem.

I love the gorgon
for her irreversible effect.

# The Stuff

Because nothing matters,
we decide what matters,
and I can think of nothing better.
Not that it matters.

If we are made of the fundamental stuff
of the universe, why *shouldn't* it respond to us?
Harder though it is, every day, to believe
the essential myth of I-will-be.

Complexity unto function is enough of a direction.
Everything that wasn't possibility has ceased,
continues to cease.  Because it wasn't possible.
Probability is a bias that brakes our heart.

We would have everything locked
and hold the key,
but it is hard to keep a key
in a kingdom of envy and avarice.

# The Manifesto of the Revelationary Army

I may not have the "right" but I have my orders.
From the Order of Righteousness.

My distrust fund is a wealth of unspent acrimony.
Rebel, surely, and be judged by that against which you choose rebellion.
Revoke the privilege of the chorus hiding behind other people's traumas.

All the fussy pissants ridiculing my fury with mellow rejoinders,
reducing my sacred rage unredressed with pedantic nitpicking—
damn their tepid blood! Drown them in a flood!

The Zombie Apocalypse happened a long time ago.
Even the most feted, stumbling under laurels, are disliked, hated,
for their implication that I'm ruined by what I don't want to know.

They exercise restraint, dare diminish my complaint,
depreciate the radius of my desire, the circumference of my desperation,
acting as though only the reasonable is feasible,

preaching that those who worship happiness will see happiness
in enlightenment rather than horror, than reduction
from the expansiveness of delusion.

I long as much for the casual destruction of enemies
as for the desperate salvation of love.

# A Little Knowledge Is My Favorite Thing

If we were aware of only one thing,
whether we were happy or not,
wouldn't we be happier?
To reduce complexity reduces reality,
or awareness of it/participation in it,
but how much reality do we want?
How much do we need?
Do we need more than we want?
Surely we do.  But we are so brief and
obsessed with the seductions of perception
that happiness is either nothing or everything
and we make concessions to the arguments
of our appetites, spilling the giggle out of our vessel
as though enjoyment were sufficient benefit.

# In The Previous Line

Past is naturally prelude
unless we hold it like a kitten
and carry it through the fire
to set down on our grave.
If you can't believe one person, it's preposterous
to claim you believe history.  Yes, we try, some of us.
We try so many things.  Permanent crisis syndrome.
But success is chance and massive redundancy.
Aggregate advance.  A range of compromise
when the moral conflicts with the practical.
The individual is an incarnation of the probable.
We must repeat what we want remembered.
What I put on the page is me
more than the "I" in the previous line.

# Poltergeists

the picaresque terrorist
is coming

we are creating his preconditions
emptying our virtuous space
to create the anger vacuum
that will pull him
from the theoretical
through potential
to us and ours
to color our hope operas
with rhetoric and blood

we pick them
we pick them off
droning our mantra of picnic cleansing
postponing collateral atonement for our
errors of presumed and eternal purity
preferential inequality
and the sanctity of unilateral
exorcisms

we fall like everything to gravity
but we must cover it with a story

# Pull the Trigger of Your Tongue

Nature isn't silent
until you kill it.
You? You
are so new.
Your creation,
almost all destruction.
You ridicule
a molecule.
You clutch accident
like accomplishment.
You back down
and bow down.
Then obsess
over concession.
If you condone it
you commit it.
The culpability
of complacency
claiming the insistence
of necessity.
The memory
of money.
Ignorance to ruin
time and again.
Survival
is minimal.
But inevitability
doesn't work for me.
Trust

the surplus.
If you see something
say something.
I dislike the lack
of didactic prophylactic.

# I Know A Secret

The status quo is strongly defended.
But truth is not answerable to the hierarchy.

Some people blow themselves up to destroy the innocent
(well, the ignorant).  Others blow a whistle to warn them.

These heroes can't be heroes if we vilify them.
They say.  Bestowing an officious stomp of disapproval.

Anyone who wants to judge me
had better stand ready to be similarly judged.

Authority that can't accept debate
has no authority.

No one is free who is denied access to facts.
Neutrality is ignorance or apathy.

We are taught to reveal atrocity (or truth concealed
among conspiracy theories) but not to accept the consequences

of sacrifice.

# Soliloquy

I crave walls built of stone, supports made to be
around a while, because I love them, not because
I buy their lie.  There's no tomorrow—well, there is,
until there isn't.  Like your body hasn't failed, until it has;
like your memory hasn't filled all the space formerly
stockpiling hope, until it has; like your identity
hasn't dissipated into a vague, opaque approximation
of unique, until...well, you know the drill.

I love them not because of their lie—not *despite* it, either—
it's incidental—I love them, rather, because of their
metaphorical weight in my anthropomorphic schema,
and because they reply to my soliloquies with echo.
Stone is old—really, really old.  It dreams of the defensible,
tastes of the sated, the assurances of repetition, a frenzy
of solitude.  But even within the enclosure, exposure.
Walls made of paper are better for poems.

# The Gelded Age

seven billion people making poetry
most in verses of silence and suffering
and labor and conflict and conformity

fatigue and complacency
producing an emotional irritability
and an intellectual drowsiness

the sameness of symmetry
the sadness of hope
the comfort of the familiar

apoplectic dilettantes
purged of romantic expectation
and the illusion that echoes renew

but not everyone insists upon the reduced
dialect a la mode nor limits their thoughts
to the broadcast mantras of muting

the accretion of haptic technology adapted for masochists
the deletion routines of augmented reality that perfect
our capacity for ignoring annoyances and undesirables

shirking the duty to suffer and be joyous
that we owe to the moss
and the weeds and the happy plankton

if all that matters
are a few years in late adolescence
then what's the point?

if it is difficult to assess
the preference
of the anonymous

why are we so good at profiling
the lowest common denominator?

# Turtles All The Way

Down.  Up.  Whichever direction
in whichever dimension.
Everything is expression,
variously expressed.
Competitive and cooperative mechanisms
work to calculate reactions.
Marvel at the aggregate.
Meaning is spurious.
Your turtle may not be expressed as turtle.
All experience is vicarious.
Consider your processes and your products.
This is enlightenment.

# is am are was were be being been

*do not fret*
*do not fret*
*everything is ending*
*but it ain't done yet*

the key to imagining a future of duration
is to admit that it will transcend your imagination
*(ah, Horatio!)*

new encounters, new satisfactions,
and yes, new wounds

those who can't, who think they own it,
will welcome extinction
to escape from an interminable parade of todays

a change in quantity (even increase)
doesn't serve when we crave a change in kind:
incremental stability

being free is being nothing
and so we enshackle ourselves for experience
with successive efforts and capitulations

even an existential materialist
should concede that material
can be formed into wonders
by a creative intelligence

your veneer, is it supple or brittle?

*do not fret*
*place your bet*
*everything is ending*
*but it ain't done yet*

# Most Love Is Tired and Cannot Sleep

Most love is tired and cannot sleep.
A life is strained, confused, a spasm.
Most dream dim in fits and starts,
awaken, shake, lose their place—
words fade, evaporate from hypnopompic pages—
forgetting everything but the strange,
the shades, recalling just a bit of face
long gone.  Again.  No material loss enrages
insomniacs or lovers like the bits and parts
that in crossing the chasm define the chasm:
nothing so wide ever seemed so deep.

# Lusus Indorum

History calculates probability;
novelty is very difficult to assess.
A today empty of yesterdays
is as void as a tomorrow.

Memories are delicate.
Too much handling
will soil—or in some cases, erase—
them.

Unconstruct
the mechanisms
of senescence.

I hate an obscurantist
be he poet or priest.
Though art is dependent upon forgetfulness,
the impatience of impotence.

A tree stump, being an authentic remnant,
is sadder than a grave, which is merely representational.
Sometimes taking things out of context
is the best way to take them.

Sometimes what appear to be transgressions
are really corrections
of prior failure.

# Elegy for Edges

The impossible is of no interest whatsoever.
The inaccessible is irresistible.

An acknowledgment of perpetual transience
leads to the development of ecstatogenic techniques,

aspiration to deprivation
abandoned for blessings of the yes-yes.

What to say to the literalist
for whom abstractions lack edges to grasp,

who prefers the limits of banal concretions
because he can count the feathers,

because the sensation of stubbing his toe allows
him to pretend a conception of his forgotten origins,

because he relishes the comforts of recognition
rather than the challenges of examining patterns?

Truth is imprisoned in a prism, fractalicious,
with facets on facets, shattered into being

with the relentless eroticism of ice
cracking rock.

The merely accommodating is much too small.

# The Spellcasters

in the center
subtleties are turned into details
and consigned to specialists,
who confine them in jargon
and hide them away, jealously-guarded

on the periphery
one eludes more of the ramifications
of rampant madness,
or believes that one does

deny the spellcasters and you are immune,
decline to incant, to cast or enchant, and you are alone

intelligence, whatever that is, depends upon autonomy,
an uncommon talent for examining everything at close range
yet pulling back to make a space for experience without interference

a passion for data can't always wait for order
and sacrifices the pleasures that accompany it
for the ongoing flow of staccato satisfactions

as knowledge increases, so will resistance to learning,
isomemetic decoherence to cope with the coercion of perception,
cycles of attention and distraction
contracting to an intermittent focus

successive renderings of identity
as imagined by the mask behind the masks

# Self-Assessment

Poems are like people:
the finite in infinite combination.

Patterns of patterns
lost in patterns,
we love truth
and other nonsense.

Pedigree is an illusion:
each of us is a new roll
of the same die,
beholden to all,
beholden to none.

We need to delve deeper
into our variability,
adulterate the purity
to investigate complexity.

I don't know what I need to know.
Can I learn fast enough not to fail?

Which is worse,
to be trivial or irrelevant?

# Butterfly Dreams

Okay,
I can see dreaming I'm a
　　{butterfly}, but
a butterfly will never,
　　can never, dream
it's a man. A caterpillar,
　　maybe, but never a
　　　　man.

Oh, it may dream itself
　　into the clumsy,
lumbering *form* of a man,

　　enormous, wingless
　　　　biped,

but it will have no point
　　of reference,
no data, to imagine,
　　much less to simulate,

the man-ness
　　　　of a man.

A man in the dream
　　of a butterfly
will be a butterfly
　　shaped like a man.

And, too, a {butterfly}
　　in the dream of a man

will be a man, always,
　　trying unsuccessfully

　　　　to subside into animal.

# Sappho Said The Most Beautiful Thing

Sappho said the most beautiful thing
is whatever one loves.
Keats' equation would indicate
that it's also the truest.
But all love is delusion.
So we are factories of false truth.

Aggregate, regulate, mitigate,
you who fear the each alone
and his and her power to slip
the dictates of conformity
to ring the bell of the rebel.

If there were more time
one wouldn't have to force things,
if there were time for them to develop naturally
or statistically.  But there is so little time
and so much that
                    we feel
should happen.

# Free Will

There is no true free will,
not any that's real,
that approaches the ideal,
the kind we think we feel,
the kind with such appeal
that we pretend it still.

But it's not a big deal.
We still do as we will.
With pretty much the same zeal.
It's just that "we" stands revealed.

# The Times, They Are Derangin'

Our only hope,
uplift over the hump
of our legacy limits.

Everybody hustling and hassling
and half-assing their way
through, trying, getting-bying,
crossing off another day.

The problem with miracles is their scarcity.
The "second harvest" of terminal lucidity.

So long as the world changes,
who can run out of things to say?

  "It's changed."
  "It's changed."
  "It's changed again."

Move too quickly, it can't provide enough variety.
Move too slowly, it can't provide enough detail.

Do we want new chapters in old narratives
or will we forever settle for new narratives,
new narrators?

Nothing that doesn't move
or want to
needs stories.

We want everything to be alive
and will bring it all to life
if we can avoid death long enough.

Those radical enough to integrate the past
are the ones to watch.

The problem with miracles is their ubiquity.
Eagerness presenting as anxiety.

# The Subterfuge

I have travelled far
I would travel further

to acquire in order
to be deprived of what I have

the racket of the rapture
of the rats

to sing things together
to stare them apart

a tactile attack
of tact

to rectify the subterfuge
from foundation to fortification

the tight delight
of ferns in urns

a critic of system
relinquished by suicides

the gift?
or the rescinding of the gift?

# An Embarrassment of Glitches

we promise ourselves false premises
we dream of effort and effect

flesh machines
for stripping life

down to mundane
foundations

we skim and scan the signs of mind
we undervalue the casual accretion

we provide instructions for mischief
we issue invitations to vandalism

from straight to strange
we  rearrange

intent and chance trying for worse...
but who can make the poems run on time?

# Manners and Maneuvers

the self-confined
the habit of no habit
the self-impoverished
the light without light
the eradication of tribes
the busywork of heroism
the chloroform of uniform
the idle necessities of power
the constant weight of thought
the complacency of the customary
the partial overlap of our vocabularies
the hot-rock drunk notoriety of sobriety
the danger of studying beyond understanding
the distance between the fugitive and the refugee
the disparate dispassionate appetites of martyrs and satyrs
the myth of the appropriate and other contractions of consciousness

# The Eroticism of Collapse

*And you, you accept them in despair,*
*these things that you don't want.*
– C. P. Cavafy, from "The Satropy"

How dare we sleep for such long stretches
with all the dangers circling our sleeping bodies?

In a democracy, everyone wants a palace and
no one wants to rule, elitists who are not part of an elite,
obsessive taxonomists fallen to unworshipped relics,
sinister leftovers, criminal vestiges,
ever mourning the world of a moment before,
contemplating the positive characteristics of a stain.

What insanity seeks symbols
in antecedents?

Faust is the favorite fantasy of the obscurantist
obsessed with orthopraxy.  It is not the alienness
of Frankenstein's monsters that is offputting,
it's the familiarity, the allure of the relentless fuckup
that will not take yes for an answer.
Or no for a question.

We don't understand their lack of understanding.
We dream descendants of their dreams.
We forget their feelings and their names.
We live different lives and die the same.
Contradictions are clues.

Miracles are things we see in a mirror, reversed.
Manifest desperation.  Time is toxic.
You may break any rule
but the rule that determines
which rules you may break.

Is the goal to operate at the boundary
of the laws of physics?

If you acknowledge the game,
you can't play the game.

# The Empathy of the Outlaw

where thieves thrive
wealth is much disputed

the salvage of savagery
solved, saved

each swearing fealty
to the seductive or the sedative

specks reckoning epic
from the legitimacy of the self-undermining

too cynical to be a foot soldier,
not cynical enough (by half) to be a general

pedestritutes
seduced by the simplicity of scarcity economics

ludicrous uses
of lucre

sentenced to life
for crimes against eternity

radiating vectors of violence
from a Trojan hearse

trapped
by the overlap

in the world they'd sell us,
kindness reeks of madness

# Screed

keep your self-deprecating angst
your exhibitionist shtick
your easy anger, your sleazy pandering

America has always been about seeing
how far one can go with a desire
(usually called "dream") and a gun

we feel without training
it is better to be a terror
than a nuisance

hobidy-boobies
trying to scare one another
and scaring themselves

and now for our next entertainment
a long-popular farce recently out of fashion—
*CIVIL WAR!*

the Party of God vs the Party of Man
vs the Party of Wealth vs the Party of Hope
vs the Party of Science vs the Party of Sense

how foolish, the one who consents
to engage with a foolish society
on its own terms!

every day I celebrate the liberty
to decline
by doing so

we are untruly represented
in government and in religion
and in the opinion of those who know us

democracy makes
a better seedbed
than guardian

# Small Gifts

We love the gun more than anyone
because it feels like a promise of justice,
and though it lies, we are used to lies
from those who promise, from those we love.
Its grip is made for our grasp, and it says
it's better to give small gifts to many
than to receive one large one, so pull it,
pull it for bullets, and share your kisses
with those who resist.

# Tongues of a Thousand Corpses

perception is weak,
interpretation strong,
fecund

our sentences are guesses
but we're constitutionally incapable
of calculating confirmation

always be suspicious
of the reasons for no,
of the rationalizations of yes,
of indecisiveness

programmed to love friction
we demand abrasion,
insist on a promiscuous purpose

even our language
has a tendency to fracture
toward tribalism

who can have
enough love
for the perfect
and imperfect?

# Logogenesis

My mind is my familiar, my totem,
my sacred thing
(the sacred doesn't have to be large).

Perception analyst, egalitarian elitist,
unfashionably sincere, suffering
a failure of assembly or of information,

sometimes I don't need to know the words for things,
I just need to know they're there—the words—if I need them
(which is often more than can be said for the things),

to find joy in complexity, electric locutions,
to attune to verbal munitions
prior to widescale deployment,

to convert my ideas to expression,
my dreams to experience,
to read—or reach—the parallels.

Rhetoric originates in the implication
of insistence, undeveloped
or subject to other defects.

The purpose of poetry is play—
*high praise!*—play has always been
more important than work.

Some are content not to produce
so long as they can play.
Others prefer it the other way.

It's best to do your sage phase
when no one knows your name,
glib mime, misled

by canary associations,
song overwritten
by sadness reaction

to cage and mine,
to anarchic chic among irascible muddlebrow imbeciles,
tacit tactics, scrutiny disguised as passionless glances,

disambiguation of the autodidact,
flippancy, not insouciance,
as the inopportune tuning of the dissonant,

the other variables,
once more beyond our reach,
requiring a stretch.

Which is stronger in the ring,
intention or perception?
Will either ever take on the champion,

Just Is?
Praise impulse over catastrophic success
calculating the impracticalities of peak poetry.

To renounce the accretions and return to the source
doesn't have to be the act of a fearful conservative heart
if one understands the source.

# Fata Morgana

There's a commotion in my continuity,
cherrypicking personality.

What could be more adaptive
than cognitive dissonance?

Reality, hallowed out.
Arbitrary.  Corollary.

The reliability of the unsteady,
the tyranny of the imaginary.

Good news
and/or a good result.

A congruence of misunderstandings,
subjectively superior equivalencies.

Familiar formulations,
similar simulations.

The things we keep
in case of need.

History is the desperate record
of the quickly-extinguished.

How much of an answer is it, really,
to cultivate obsessions?

Is it courage or pride
that dares interrupt light?

# Inadequate Sign

The mechanism for securing or scouring data
is the basis of sequential processing, of life,
is how we model intent from inadequate sign,
cataloging the discoveries of ego, the inventions of desire,
the application of lore acquired long before,
assimilated in the service of inquiry.

*Ladies and gentlemen, start your ingenuity!*

My strongest influences are my earlier selves.
I'm not quite done with them.

The excessively-used, the new—I lay claim to all of it,
a lifetime replete with wonders and horrors,
will need all of it to make sense.

How essential *is* personality?
Is it just a tool, a convenience, a comfort?

Is seeking to side-step or dismiss the illusion
movement toward or away from sanity?

At a certain age one develops a sixth sense for entropy;
it becomes as personal and inescapable as vision in youth,
every perception of the world is filtered through it
and comes out drained.

There may come a time when you've seen everything
and just not registered it consciously; going forward,
every discovery may be a memory.

I shall always kiss the blasphemous face:
what is precious can withstand any assault
but violence; what is not
I don't want.

# Valentine

Men play Janus
because women worship Proteus.

What have we not done to one another?
How futile is my refusal to be a part of it?

Who is content with the love of strangers?
They're all strangers.

The moon would say she's the sun's lover
because he shines so much light on her.

More stars than can be counted,
but more empty space between them.

# Paradigm Shift

I have seen mummies sleeping
and voodoo frauds,
the almost-sexual appeal of trinkets,
both tool and toy.

Every society will reward you
if you agree to its deceits
(though they may not be
the redemptive rewards you anticipate
when you capitulate).

Competitive frivolities,
coercive frailties.

The first squirt of blood shocks the world
more than a sea of it.

I grow tired of breathing society's exhaust.

Wealth lies in superfluity.
Historic impoverishment
is inevitable now.

And of the not-young in their mocking chairs
craving the hemlock
with petulant cigarettes
saying

"Stoke me with resentments,
prime me with resistance,
and I shall sputter and smoke on schedule."

# Universal Translator

I speak in my language; you listen for yours.

Striving to cull the crosslinking false cognates
which sing near valid inside and infiltrate,
we co-opt words from the private lives of our antecedents,
inscribe definitions into the abridged dictionaries of our requirements.

We exhale inert inquiring idioms until the small djinn
of misunderstanding pass enough confused whispers
to make recognition plausible.

But what is said is weighted down with approval
so it can't leak secrets or surprise with truth,
can't work to convert the unknown into the familiar.

The wisest things you ever said to me
you didn't hear.

# Critic

Sometimes I feel I'm going sane,
subterranean.
I am adequately bermed
like indolent endomorphs
by my own pleasure-less leisure—
*it can't hurt if it doesn't hit*—
though few would thank me
for the taint of my endorsement
(best is not always most pleasant).
Celebrations of correlation and conformity
interrupt the unexpected hunt for charlatans—
conspiracy of the arbiters.
Even the insipid need insulin—
goodnight, sweet prints.

# Critic 2

humans cherish
the illusion of inevitability

looking back
at one's trail of crumbs

temples and shrines of unknown origin
of lost purpose

subdivide the indivisible
with missionary arrogance

acquisition is an inquisition
of value

differences can be substantial
and yet superficial

a value of power
requires its square of wisdom

the opposite of the neurotic
is a critic of the ecstatic

restoration requires reflection
as well as loss

# Talisman

What ways we find
to convince ourselves
and others that we matter!

At most levels of scale
the truth is, we don't.

But across a narrow,
precious spectrum,
we do.

People don't love talismans
for their efficacy.

Participation
promotes delusions
of belonging.

Why aren't we trained
to react heroically,

to measure
the resistance of the world
to intent and effort?

Replace dogma with dogma,
and what have you done?

# The Wisdom of the Crowd

*While in the street*
*outside, the people hear nothing at all.*
– C. P. Cavafy, from "But Wise Men
Apprehend What Is Imminent"

If we mattered
we'd have more time.

The day comes
when we will eagerly trade the past
for more tomorrow.

Not so much chosen
as the result of our choices,

the wild world
violating our timid wills with rhythm,
a blow exchanged for a blow.

How else can we treat the stranger,
believing ourselves what we believe ourselves?

Must we fill the moat with trash, tear down every stone
that sits on stone, and move into temporary shelters,
tents and cardboard boxes?

The best scripts are written after the curtain comes down.
We love neither chance nor the inevitable.
The Poem of Forgetting remains so much more popular,
so much more familiar than the Poem of Remembering.
Choose: Wandering or searching?

# Dream

In the grocery store
I found a sheet cake
with a real poem
written on it in frosting.

I read it aloud
and it was the best reading of my life
despite the critical remarks
of a nearby woman.

I felt it faltered somewhat
at the end
when it namechecked
several other poets.

The best line
that I remember
was "Give,
then forget it."

I took the cake
to another aisle,
made sure I was alone,
then left it on a shelf

and hurried back to my cart.

# The Flaw

I saw the flaw


one erodes like a riverbank
but is not always resilted so


gratitude is an attitude
the urge is rage


she betrayed you
he failed you


the satisfaction of anger
doesn't resolve


focus lingers into obsession


how do you let someone know
there is an insufficiency?


power is a zero-sum game
limited by opportunities for control


how many variables are required
to establish uniqueness?


repulse the compulsion
to differentiate on trivia

to privilege the already-known
with a credibility head-start

heresy isn't always truth
but neither is doctrine

the price of dialogue is engagement
participation trades authority for influence

speculation without confirmation
is what leads to madness

facts, no matter how unexpected,
can be assimilated

expectations, no matter how true,
are flawed

# Dissensus

Is everything, anything significant?
Is anything, everything important?

One thing is always like another,
we just don't always know how.

We live in a Fippy Darkpaw world.
You'll say we don't—but look
harder, we do.

Changing what you say is one option.
Changing what you mean when you say what you say is another.

I think that I shall never see
a poem as lovely as a poem.

Do you want to be serious
or do you want to be sincere, they ask me.

The best you can hope for is that others take you seriously?

Put a price on dignity
and people will line up to cash in.

You can't persuade me
to be as small as culture,
to habituate to the illusions
of unity, sanity, security—
you can threaten me
but I'm not listening.

When did I decide that I needed adversaries?
When did I stop believing in friends?

# The Criteria

At what point
do you disbelieve everything?
For the sake of argument,
for the sake of agreement,
we should consider the criteria
for establishing the parameters.
Because, look.
I mean, look!
Isn't there an inherent
obligation to ridicule the ridiculous?
Or should we pretend
to be entertained
until the very end?
I suspect I prefer
a content continuance
over a happy ending.
And a blunt denial
over polite pretending.
Nothing is what it seems:
everything deconstructs into dreams.

# Global Warming

The world burns without me.

The firemen are on strike
because they are not thanked often enough
for their sacrifice.
The best friends of your childhood
become the worst enemies of your maturity.
Bruno felt the coming of the flames
that are now arrived.

As a kid, I got along well with clouds
and loved the sea.
Now the water fuels the fire.
"Only you can prevent..."
But you can't.  You can't.
The world burns without you.

The scientists are on strike
because everyone was too busy
making love and money
to listen to them.
Now they are down at the bar
with the firemen, drinking
the last of the cold beer and
comparing sacrifices they have made
in the face of ingratitude,
saying "Let the dead burn
on their pyres without us."

But you can't.  You can't.

# The Metacognitive Deficit

We are our answered questions about ourselves.
We are our unanswered questions about ourselves.

Admire my nonadvantageous epiphenomena!
Listen to my nonrandom hypotheses!

What can we exapt from what we've found?
What can we pervert into new facility?

Can we be content with free will
as epiphenomenon of determined processes?

What kind of trade imbalance
do our imports and exports negotiate?

I feel a degradation of fidelity—
how many times have I been copied?

We are others' questions about us,
but we are not their answers.

# Emphasis

society has some funny ideas
it's forgotten how to laugh at

if consent is weak,
what is critique?

difference is a matter
of emphasis

I reject awe,
prefer delight

of the free things I will borrow
any and all without restriction

stitching bits
for practicality and fashion

once coddled,
we cultivate distress

a siren sonata
alarm album

no other music
seems relevant now

to be something
say something

I've nostalgia for how
words were used

in my youth

# The Fixed Function

An egret or crane may prompt us to thought,
but it doesn't matter *which* crane or egret;
they all work the same, as symbols, not individuals,
and have for thousands of years;

the same thought
for so many people
who we insist it matters
were different.

# Slogan's Heroes

I look for holy ground
to support my holy feet,
engage my holy looking,
and discover that all ground is holy
that hasn't been desanctified
by human malignity
or carelessness.

You look long and hard for someone to tell you what you want to hear—
*and how hard it is to take them seriously!*—
and then they stop saying the kind of thing you like
and start saying the kind of thing that's not your thing.

We are told again and again of horrors
not so we'll recognize them, defend against them,
but so they'll become common and slip
beneath our threshold of recognition,
so they can move among us
and position themselves against us
without suffering the notice and exposure of novelty.

People generally choose violence over boredom.
Small people fight for their country, for tradition,
for the interests of their masters.
God hates flags.  Or would.
If you're going to fight, fight for everything.
Forbidden our fists, anger becomes angst.

We've never had to see the world as fragile—
we were the fragile ones, and the world was forever.
Now we buy the commercialization of our narratives,
even our narratives of capitulation.
There is no greater debasement than to provide
your enemies' weapons, except doing it for profit.

Love it or fear it,
but you can't love what you fear
(though you can love the fear).
Every ordeal is a bad deal
no matter what benefit we might wrest from it.

# The Golden Blade of the Terror Trade

The guillotine follows optimism
like a gypsy curse.  What
cannot be sustained is what
we persist in trying to sustain.

Numbed with need,
damned with hope,
we worship promise.

And tumble again and again,
our heads severed from our hearts

like procrastinating prostitutes.

# Febricula

Someday, they promised,
you will miss nostalgia.

Following a torch song
into the dark.

What we choose to remember of history
condemns us.

Memory is inadequate,
and the world won't remember for us.

Adaptation is neither victory nor failure.
What, then, is it?

Choice? or action?
Again I can't decide.

The future kills the present,
moment by moment.

# Genocidesis

What the enemy sells is not the dark
but the opaque, which can't be cured
by light alone.

The consumption of fire tribes,
the cycle-time of earth tribes.

The world, stingy with souvenirs,
knowing their worth
but not the need that seeks them.

A luckbeast, lurking and passing
and making itself scarce
among incongruities of context,

alogical inquiries, and aesthetic attacks,
the conundrum of quondam mechanics,
rigorous surveillance of so-called history,

the truth, so much less treasured than utility,
muddled in puddles of the inevitable,
signals triggered by figments

trying so hard to embody ourselves,
to make artifice of ephemera,
writing elegies to eulogies.

And I believed
we said what others have said
to learn to say what no one has said.

The amnesia of wind tribes,
the erosion of water tribes.

And still I remain open
to revelations
of a new suffering.

# Slipping

It's okay
that new stories
replace forgotten myths.

Abstraction and the concrete:
which is figure and which is ground?
Or is it a yin-yang thing?

We are
the answers
of our ancestors.

Feverish with
the futility of temporary,
the desperation of now.

Nails on a blackboard,
that is our grip on our lives,
slipping.

Sometimes I want to be loose
and sometimes I want to be tight—
isn't that right?

Possibility
trimmed and severed
by decision.

My guesses:  haphazard light
reflected from clusters of mica and pyrite,
briefly illuminating neglected quantities of quartz.

Houses aren't haunted,
people are.
But who wants to admit *that*?

# Proverb

What shadow makes clear are the limits of light.
Our ancestors' anthems, our lullabies.

Sages don't have the best answers.
They have the best questions.

It's a narcissistic reading of Narcissus
that doesn't acknowledge the fascination of water.

Enough money to fill a shed, and then
burning the shed to release the sacred fire.

How much it would have meant
when it still mattered!

And yet so many marvels left unborn
without wealth to birth them.

Even the lying Bible, embracing heresies faster than they
could be devised, admits that God is a maker, not a father.

# Stratagem

There is a time for litany—
this isn't it.

Catastrophes cure stasis,
stagnation and bliss.

Sometimes I do.
But even when I do I don't.

All my reality checks bounced
due to insufficient fun.

Difference matters.  Does sameness?
Free will is so expensive.

Memory is an intermediate state
between notice and myth.

Learn to love what you've lost
and you'll love forever.

# Litany

I am <list of things I am, including some surprising inclusions>
I am not <list of denials, some improbable and unpersuasive>
I am a little of this
and a lot of those others
I am this and I am that, both and neither
I am a we and a nobody
I am except when I am not
I am not, only occasionally I am
I am trying to be (but already am)
I am the trying, it seems, more than the being
I am what I can and
I am what I can't
I am not what they say I am
I am not what I say I am
I am parts unknown to other parts
Even Descartes gets me wrong
I am a residual process of cooperation
seeking wholeness in the emptiness of every moment

# Cold

I used to get so cold.
Sometimes I would snatch
nearby rats, snap
their necks, and
line my blankets
with their twitching
bodies for the fading
heat.

I still got cold.

I still get cold.

# Every Body

How long till your drones
chase the birds of the sky
to set them on fire?

How long till you put a bullet
in every body that needs one?

We are visionary fugitives,
reading romanticism as irony
and realism as myopia.

We are the same and different
in ways different than you claim.

# Sex

has brought on a climatic event,
given us little organisms
dying little deaths
all over the planet.

We didn't plan it,
one thing led to another,
it just happened—
maybe we were drunk?

And now we're sunk.

# The Elephant

The elephant in the room
is that for the people of the future
the elephant in the room
is that there is no elephant
in or outside of their room
because of us.

Instead of bequeathing them an elephant
to impoverish them a la the King of Thailand of old,
we bequeath them *no elephant* to impoverish them.

I'd like to think they'll never forgive us
our selfish dyscalculia, but I know
it won't even come to that:
they'll forget us instead
and our efforts to cheapen experience
enough to be able to afford it.

We resent history because it's immune to us.
We adore only what we destroy.
We are a match,
not a torch.

# Funambulists

you'd think
by now
we'd get more right
than we do
you'd think improvements
hard as consistency
easy as dream
would evidence
and propel us into love
or a more reasonable alternative
but here we are
screwing up
screwing each other
and ourselves
and sufficiently content
to make do with complaint
at first and then regret
bookends to disappointment

# Give Our Titles, Our Texts,
# A Purpose Beyond Marketing

All we can know is data.
Even the interpretation of data is data.

Stranger, give me a trajectory
and estimate of duration,
and I will launch at the target
my entire composition.

I will not assume
as a tactic of contingency or conclusion
the tiresome glory, the glorious tedium
of the epic.

A different result requires a different input.
Or different conditions.
Or an intervention of chance.

Comparison is safe;
it's contrast that can be deadly.

Around the time we change from coming to going,
we begin to think it strange how little time for being.

# The Lion in Ruin

The lion eroded into jackal—
There's just no denying—
And it's impossible to tell
When or how or why,
Whether all lions have jackals inside
(Or maybe only some?)
Or whether jackals just arrive
When lions die.

# The Shape of the Smoke

Change would eventually steal everyone from you anyway.
But they'd still be.  Out there.  Becoming.
Lost to you, yes, but not annihilated.

Conservation of energy is not enough.
Conservation of identity.
But illusions exist only in their effect.
Time is the wind (blowing, blowing)
that disrupts, dissipates the apparent shape
of the smoke.

But what was burning?

# Then and Now

The humanist's plea: "May everyone get no worse than they deserve."
Expectation is not the cure for surprise that you'd think it'd be.
Being affected by everything doesn't mean you are interconnected.
Wouldn't interconnectedness require independence?
Otherwise what you're looking at is unity.
It is the easiest hard thing in the world to release,
to relinquish something—the only thing that stops us is us.
You've overcomplicated things if you've found yourself back at
    appeasement.
Is it a miscalculation when you never bothered to do the math?
The purpose of society is to mix everything together.
The purpose of the individual is to pull from the mix a suitable
    selection.
To what extent can we distinguish difference to ourselves, never
    mind others,
without words?  Even happy memories have a sadness to them,
encoded as they are with the gap between then and now.

# Still Life

In the anarchic cloister,
the forever endeavor

to feel things differently
or to feel different things.

All sacrifice is tainted,
all offerings spoiled

in the striving toward relevance
of the initially incidental.

We continue wobbling
under illusions of stability,

deceived by the serendipity
of neutral intention,

our difference-detectors'
tendency to err,

progress missed
in silly stillness.

A convocation, a cavalcade,
responsibilities compromised by desire,

ethics redacted
from documented relations,

hot-and-bothered by ins and outs,
inevitable ironies, self-fulfilling ironies,

erratic eroticism
using the similar to illuminate the different,

rejecting names, basking in
the immediacy of presence.

It's still life.

# Inertials vs. the Randomites

Distrust society's assessments.
They are dishonest.

What is pity without understanding
but an insult from an unmelted self?

We became bad when we invented bad.
Erosion accelerates on the excavated.

Is there any greater commitment
than the commitment to keeping your options open?

See what we can do with our hands untied?
See what we can do with our mouths untaped?

Why do you approach us now with rope and tape?

# Being Human

a man stands
deep at the bottom
of a dry well

his enemies
(and a few of his friends)
throw stones down
while he looks up
and dodges

eventually he
could climb out
if only they would agree
to drop them
one at a time

# All You Love Is Need

*My Eros is crucified.*
                                    – St. Ignatius

*...so don't mess around,*
*don't mess around with me.*
                                    – Elvis

I chose poorly.
Friends.  Lovers.  Others.
Chose more carefully
if less often
than anyone I know—*terrible!*
My habitual ideas
slowly poisoning me.
I didn't learn a thing about taking
joy in measured extravagance.
The only unwise love is to love
him or her who cannot love.
All psychology is probability.
Failure may be guaranteed.
What they don't tell you
(but you should have known)
is that Plato's fire
is love.
So now what?

# I Got Words

I wanted love—
I got words.

I wanted adventure—
I got words.

I wanted knowledge—
I got words.

I wanted health and other wealth—
I got words.

I wanted everything.
I got words.

I got words.

# The Realm

There is a realm
that's claimed me as its poet,
but I can't get there from here.
It's far.
They hold feasts in my name,
eat fruit and drink nectar,
and the light from the stars
brightens blank pages they wait
to see darken with my poems.
I've everything they need here,
and they've everything I want, there.
I write.  They wait.
The gap's to blame.

# Origami

Tomorrow I'll find the pond
and watch the paper fish
spin across the stagnant water,
sog, and sink to the bottom.
I'll see the clever old kids
kneeling in their paper overalls,
cutting out paper fish
from discarded computer print-outs,
and count the silent schools
that line the shallow fountain
like acid-washed leaves or
freakish snowflakes that won't melt.
I will fish in my pockets,
those empty folds in starched paper,
and wish for crumbs I threw away
when there were loaves to spare.

# Drifting Free

I rather think the life I know
is like the iceberg parts that show—
the cold wind-twisted bits that melt
and freeze again, the fury felt—
yet within and deep below
the ice is blue and clear of snow
and will not melt or change at all
till warmer waters force a thaw.
Drifting free, I wonder though,
if all the sea's a frigid flow.

# Dying

Those who shouted defiance at death have died.
I honor them.  At least they tried.
Better than those who pretend
that a beginning requires an end.
Life prepares for death by weakening you,
the wounded being easier to subdue.
Dying, dying, dying.
But at least we're trying.

# Lying in the Gregarium

There is no obligation to interact with others.
It can help.
It will also make things harder.
Another choice you must make for yourself.

The vanity of love or the inhumanity of indifference?
Little wonder we've become masters of obfuscation.

Without the tyranny of desire
we would subside into egalitarian nonbeing.
The question is, would this be a good thing or not?

I would fight so hard to remain myself
if I knew what I was fighting for.

The only cure for curiosity is truth.
No fiction will suffice.
Not even happiness.

The answer is in the last place I will look.